from SEA TO SHINING SEA

IDAHO

By Dennis Brindell Fradin

CONSULTANTS

Merle Wells, Ph.D., Staff Historian, Idaho State Historical Society

Robert L. Hillerich, Ph.D., Professor Emeritus, Bowling Green State University;
Consultant, Pinellas County Schools, Florida

CHILDRENS PRESS®
CHICAGO

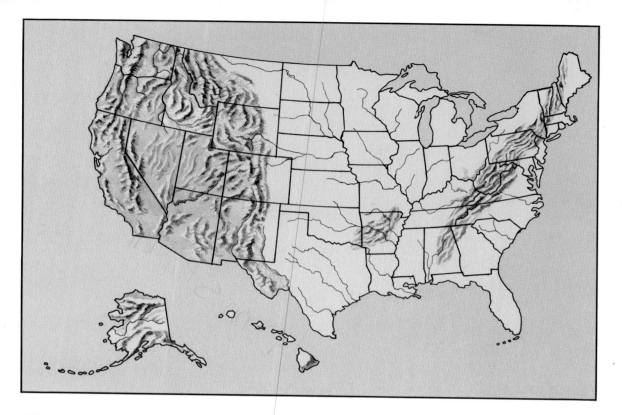

Idaho is one of the six Rocky Mountain states. The other Rocky Mountain states are Colorado, Montana, Nevada, Utah, and Wyoming.

For the children and faculty of West School in Glencoe, Illinois

For their help, the author thanks Kathy Kestner, community services librarian, Lewiston City Library; Gayle G. Wray, librarian, Legislative Services Office, State Capitol, Boise; Boise Public Library; Elizabeth Jacox, Idaho State Historical Society Library and Archives

Front cover picture: Hells Canyon National Wildlife Refuge; page 1: fields of canola in Swan Valley; back cover: Upper Mesa Falls on the Snake River

Project Editor: Joan Downing
Design Director: Karen Kohn
Research Assistant: Judith Bloom Fradin
Typesetting: Graphic Connections, Inc.
Engraving: Liberty Photoengraving

Library of Congress Cataloging-in-Publication Data

Fradin, Dennis B.
  Idaho / by Dennis Brindell Fradin.
    p.   cm. — (From sea to shining sea)
  Includes index.
  ISBN 0-516-03812-5
  1. Idaho—Juvenile literature. [1. Idaho.] I. Title.
II. Series: Fradin, Dennis B. From sea to shining sea.
F746.3.F7   1995   95-2693
979.6—dc20   CIP
                                              AC

Table of Contents

Children enjoying a hayride at the McCall Winter Carnival

INTRODUCING THE GEM STATE

*I*daho is in the northwestern part of the United States. Mountains, lakes, and rivers give Idaho a rugged beauty. Until 1805, American Indians had Idaho's beauty to themselves. In that year, the Lewis and Clark Expedition reached present-day Idaho. Soon, fur traders, miners, and farmers came to Idaho.

One of Idaho's nicknames is the "Gem State." Today, the state is a leader in mining silver. Gold, lead, and garnets and other gems are also mined there. Another nickname is the "Spud State." It is also famous for growing potatoes. No other state grows nearly as many. Idaho is also a top grower of barley, sugar beets, and plums. Food packing and logging are among the state's main industries.

Idaho is a gem of a state in other ways, too. Where were author Carol Ryrie Brink and baseball's Harmon Killebrew born? Which state has Craters of the Moon National Monument and Sun Valley? Which state has the country's deepest canyon? Where is the world's first town to be lighted with nuclear energy? The answer to these questions is: Idaho!

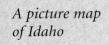

*A picture map
of Idaho*

*Overleaf: Expansive
prairie near Camas*

5

A Land of Rivers, Lakes, and Mountains

A LAND OF RIVERS, LAKES, AND MOUNTAINS

On a map, Idaho is shaped like a mountain peak. The Gem State is one of the Rocky Mountain states. Idaho covers nearly 84,000 square miles in the Rockies. Four other Rocky Mountain states form Idaho's eastern and southern borders. Montana and Wyoming are to the east. Utah and Nevada lie to the south. Oregon and Washington are to the west. The country of Canada is to the north.

Only twelve of the other forty-nine states are larger than Idaho.

Right: Wildflowers blooming at Summit Creek, in the Pioneer Mountains

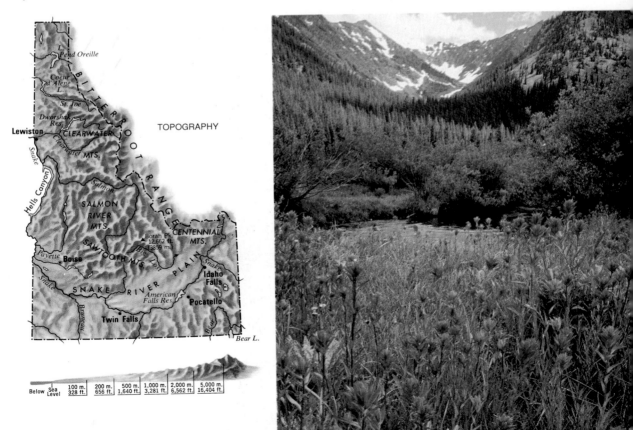

TOPOGRAPHY

Below Sea Level	100 m. 328 ft.	200 m. 656 ft.	500 m. 1,640 ft.	1,000 m. 3,281 ft.	2,000 m. 6,562 ft.	5,000 m. 16,404 ft.

*Left: Wheat and
canola fields, at
Nezperce
Right: Shoshone Falls*

The Rocky Mountains cover much of Idaho. That is why Idaho's land averages 5,000 feet above sea level. Only five states are higher. Borah Peak is the state's highest mountain. It towers 12,662 feet above sea level. That's nearly 2.5 miles high. Large deposits of silver, lead, and gold are in Idaho's Rockies.

The Columbia Plateau stretches across a large part of southern Idaho. Cattle and sheep graze on its grasses. Farmers grow potatoes, sugar beets, and fruits in its rich soil.

WATERS, WOODS, AND WILDLIFE

Idaho has more than 2,000 lakes. Lake Pend Oreille is the largest. It covers about 180 square miles. Some Idaho lakes were formed by dams on rivers. American Falls Reservoir is the biggest of these lakes. It's about 90 square miles in size.

Southern Idaho is known for its mineral springs. These waters bubble out of the ground. They form pools or ponds. Some are ice cold. Others are very hot. Soda Springs is famous for its geyser. Warm Springs is at Boise. Russian Hot Springs is near Ketchum.

The Snake River is 1,040 miles long. From Wyoming, it twists through southern Idaho. It then forms part of the state's western border before entering Washington. The 420-mile Salmon River is the longest river completely in Idaho. The Salmon is called the "River of No Return." Only jet-powered boats can travel upstream against its strong currents. Hundreds of waterfalls lie along Idaho's rivers. Shoshone Falls, on the Snake River, has a drop of 212 feet.

Early settlers boiled their eggs in Idaho's hot springs. Today, many people consider it healthful to bathe in the springs' waters.

Autumn colors at Palisades Reservoir

Trumpeter swans

Idaho is four-tenths wooded. Thick pine forests grow in the Gem State. The western white pine is the state tree. Yellow pines are also widespread. Douglas firs, white firs, and spruces are other Idaho trees. Willows, maples, birches, and cottonwoods also grow in Idaho. In warm weather, wildflowers color Idaho meadows and mountains. From afar, fields of blue camas blossoms look like lakes. The syringa, a mock orange, is the state flower. It has fragrant white blossoms.

Black bears, grizzly bears, bobcats, and coyotes roam Idaho. So do moose, white-tailed deer, and elk. Mountain goats blend in with the snow in Idaho's highlands. Mountain lions hunt bighorn sheep, and even porcupines. Salmon and trout swim in Idaho waters. The cutthroat trout is the state fish. The mountain bluebird is the state bird. More than 350 other kinds of birds fly about Idaho. They include calliope hummingbirds, golden eagles, bald eagles, hawks, falcons, trumpeter swans, and great blue herons.

CLIMATE

For a state so far north, Idaho has a mild climate. Winds off the Pacific Ocean help warm Idaho in

the winter. Mountains to the east block much cold Canadian air from entering Idaho. Winter temperatures often top 35 or 40 degrees Fahrenheit in settled parts of Idaho. In summertime, 90-degree-Fahrenheit temperatures are common.

Some parts of Idaho are desertlike. They receive only a few inches of rain a year. Idaho as a whole receives about 20 inches of rain a year. Snowfall averages about 60 inches a year in some areas. Places in some mountains have received over 30 feet of snow. Arid areas get little or no snow in most winters.

Bruneau Dunes

Temperatures fall quite a bit at night.

Overleaf: The Uhlenkott farm in the early 1900s

From Ancient Times Until Today

FROM ANCIENT TIMES UNTIL TODAY

Millions of years ago, Idaho's land took shape. Giant walls of rock pushed up from inside the earth. They became Idaho's Rocky Mountains. Volcanoes erupted. They poured out hot liquid rock called lava. About 2 million years ago, glaciers covered small parts of Idaho. As these huge sheets moved south, they cut valleys in the mountains. When the glaciers blocked valleys, huge lakes formed.

AMERICAN INDIANS

The first people reached Idaho perhaps 15,000 years ago. These early Idahoans lived in caves and rock homes. They hunted mammoths and other animals that have disappeared. Their stone tools and pottery have been found. So have their carvings and drawings on rocks. Today, rock art can be seen at Hells Canyon National Recreation Area and many other places.

Over time, many American Indian groups settled in Idaho. The Nez Percé and Shoshone were the largest groups. The Bannock, Pend d'Oreille,

Pictographs (rock drawings) along the Snake River

14

The Idaho Nez Percé lived in tepees, which were cone-shaped tents made of animal skins.

Kootenai, and Coeur d'Alene were other groups. Some Idaho Indians lived in tepees. These cone-shaped tents were made of animal skins. Other Indians built huts or dug homes into hillsides. The Indians fished for salmon and trout. They hunted deer, elk, bear, buffalo, ducks, and geese. They made cakes from camas bulbs. They made soap from the leaves of the syringa plant.

Spanish explorers brought horses to North America in the 1500s. Through trade, Idaho Indians received horses from southwestern Indians in Spanish-owned land. The Shoshone became great riders. The Nez Percé bred a strong spotted horse. These horses are called Appaloosas.

The Lewis and Clark expedition, with Sacagawea, arrived in Idaho in 1805.

Many of the fur traders and trappers were called mountain men. They came from the United States and Canada.

EXPLORERS, TRADERS, AND MISSIONARIES

Idaho was the last of the present-day fifty states visited by non-Indians. Meriwether Lewis and William Clark arrived in 1805. They were exploring the Northwest for the United States. Sacagawea came with Idaho's first non-Indian explorers. She was a young Idaho Shoshone woman. Lewis and Clark reported that Idaho had beavers and other fur-bearing animals. Furs were then in demand for making hats and other clothing.

Trappers and traders followed Lewis and Clark into Idaho. Some traveled the Rockies trapping animals. Others received furs in trade with the Indians. Fur-trading companies set up posts in Idaho. David Thompson was with the North West Company. This was an English fur company in Canada. In 1809, Thompson's men built Kullyspell House along Lake Pend Oreille. This fur-trading post was Idaho's first non-Indian building. Two other trading posts were begun in Idaho in 1834. Nathaniel Wyeth, an American, built Fort Hall in southeast Idaho. Thomas McKay was with the Hudson's Bay Company. This was another English company in Canada. McKay built Fort Boise.

During these years, Idaho was part of the Oregon country. Both the United States and England claimed that land. In 1846, England withdrew its claims. What are now Idaho, Washington, and Oregon became part of the United States.

By the mid-1830s, the fur market had fallen off. New people came to Idaho. They planned to make it their home. Reverend Henry Spalding and his wife Eliza arrived in 1836. The Spaldings were missionaries. They settled near present-day Lewiston. There they taught the Indians about Christianity. Other missionaries followed. Father Pierre-Jean De Smet was a Catholic priest. In 1842, he began a mission in far northern Idaho. Mormons from Utah

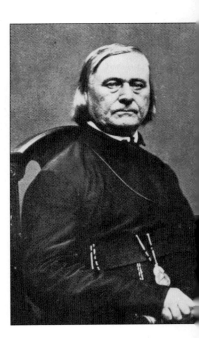

Father Pierre-Jean De Smet (above) began an Idaho mission in 1842.

settled Lemhi in 1855. Hard times forced them to leave. Another Mormon group began Franklin in 1860. Today, Franklin is Idaho's oldest town.

MINERS, FARMERS, AND INDIAN WARS

In 1860, Elias Pierce led gold seekers into northern Idaho. They found gold at Orofino Creek. Gold was soon found elsewhere in Idaho. Thousands of gold hunters poured in. Boise and Lewiston were two towns that grew because of gold mining. Idaho's early gold rushes lasted about ten years. Other kinds of mining followed. But Idaho had another treasure—rich farmland. In 1862, the United States government passed the Homestead Act. It offered free land to people who settled the West. Many former miners and families from the East built farms in Idaho.

Since the 1840s, American settlers had followed the Oregon Trail through Idaho. They were on their way to settle land in Oregon. In the early 1860s, Indians sometimes attacked these travelers in Idaho. Colonel Patrick Connor led soldiers into southeast Idaho. They attacked a Shoshone camp in January 1863. This is known as the Bear River Massacre. Nearly 400 Indians, including women and children, were killed. It was one of the worst slaughters of Indians in United States history.

On March 4, 1863, the United States government made Idaho a territory. The government made treaties with some Idaho Indian groups. Those Indians moved to reservations. Other Idaho Indians refused to be placed on reservations. This led to wars between Indians and white people in Idaho. The Nez Percé fought United States soldiers in 1877. At first, the Nez Percé had victories. Then they were forced to retreat. Under Chief Joseph, they fled toward Canada. They were stopped at the

Nez Percé leader Chief Joseph

Canadian border in Montana. Today, most Nez Percé live on Idaho's Nez Perce Reservation.

The Bannock Indians rose up in 1878. They were living on a reservation but didn't have enough to eat. United States troops defeated them that same year. In 1879, the Sheepeaters (a Shoshone group) were wrongly blamed for the deaths of five miners. They held off the army for several months before giving up. That marked the end of major fighting between Indians and whites in Idaho. Both the Bannock and Sheepeaters were sent to Idaho's Fort Hall Reservation.

In the 1880s, settlers claimed former Indian lands. Miners found silver, lead, and zinc in Idaho during those years. By 1890, Idaho had 88,548 people. That was enough for statehood. On July 3, 1890, Idaho became the forty-third state. George Shoup was Idaho's first governor.

STRIKES, FIRES, DEPRESSION, WORLD WARS

By 1890, big companies owned most Idaho mines. The miners worked hard for low pay. To improve their lives, the miners joined a union. It was called the Western Federation of Miners. In the 1890s, union miners went on strikes. Fights broke out

between miners and mine owners. There were shootings and even bombings. In 1899, Governor Frank Steunenberg depended on United States soldiers to stop the fighting. Hundreds of miners were put in prison camps. In 1905, a miner rigged a bomb that killed former governor Steunenberg. Over time, the miners gained better pay and working conditions.

Lumber companies came to Idaho in the early 1900s. Idaho became a major logging state. But in 1910, a huge fire whipped through Idaho's forests. It was one of the biggest forest fires in United States history. About eighty-five people were killed.

Idaho became a major logging state in the early 1900s.

Moses Alexander

Idaho farmers were also having trouble. Parts of their state were too dry for farming. A plan was made to irrigate the dry land. Dams, lakes, and canals were built. One dam was Arrowrock Dam. It was completed on the Boise River in 1915. The dams held back river water and formed lakes. Then, canals were dug. Water from the lakes flowed through the canals to the dry farmland. This irrigation helped Idaho's farmers grow potatoes and other crops.

Moses Alexander served as governor from 1915 to 1919. He was the first Jewish person elected as a full-term governor in any state. Alexander started a highway-building plan. He won higher wages and shorter workdays for Idahoans. In 1917, the United States entered World War I (1914-1918). Idaho sent 22,000 troops to help win the war.

The Great Depression (1929-1939) brought hardship to the United States. Idaho farmers, loggers, and miners suffered greatly. Between 1929 and 1932, Idahoans' incomes were sliced in half. The United States government set up programs. They helped people make it through the depression. Idahoans were put to work building bridges and roads and planting trees. One depression program brought electricity to farms. It was called the Rural

Electrification Administration (REA). Idaho received more REA funds than any other state.

World War II (1939-1945) helped end the depression. Japan's bombing of Pearl Harbor brought the United States into the war (1941). In 1942, the United States government forced Japanese Americans into fenced camps. The government feared that they would help Japan. One camp was the Minidoka Camp near Minidoka, Idaho. About 10,000 Japanese Americans were kept there. When given the chance, however, Japanese Americans fought bravely for the United States. About 65,000 Idaho men and women were sent off to the war. Idaho foods and metals also helped win the war.

MODERN TIMES

The end of World War II was the beginning of the Atomic Age. In 1945, the United States dropped two atomic bombs on Japan. Soon the country found peaceful uses for atomic energy. Idaho played a key role. The National Reactor Testing Station was set up near Arco in 1949. Nuclear reactors were made and tested there. These devices use atomic power to produce electricity. The testing station's

Today, most of Idaho's electricity is generated by waterpower from power plants at dams.

Japanese American women in a class at the Minidoka Relocation Center during World War II

In 1955, Arco became the world's first town lighted by nuclear energy.

23

The Sunshine Mine Memorial

work helped to provide electricity to many United States cities.

Several disasters have hit Idaho in recent times. Fire struck the Sunshine Silver Mine near Kellogg in 1972. It was one of the worst mining accidents in United States history. Ninety-one people died. Four years later, eastern Idaho's Teton Dam burst. A flood resulted. There were eleven deaths and $500 million in damages. Drought struck Idaho in 1987-1988. The lack of rain killed farm crops. In 1994, Idaho suffered one of its worst forest fires.

Idaho's salmon are also in trouble. Just 100 years ago, millions of salmon lived in Idaho waters. Each year, the adult fish would swim hundreds of miles up Idaho's rivers. They would then breed in the lakes and streams where they had been born. Today, dams on Idaho rivers prevent these fish from returning home. Redfish Lake was named for the color of the sockeye salmon. The lake was full of them each fall. In 1991, only four salmon made it back to Redfish Lake. That year, the sockeye salmon became an endangered species. Today, there are few salmon in the Salmon River.

Idahoans have been working to make their state a better place to live. The Boise River was polluted for many years. Sawmills and meat-packing plants

dumped their wastes into the river. Today, the river is clean enough to swim in. Large parks lie on both sides of the river. Business in the state capital has also boomed. Computer, lumber, and food companies have offices there. Since 1970, Boise's population has almost doubled.

On July 3, 1990, the Gem State turned 100 years old. That year Idaho's population topped 1 million. Idaho is expected to have 1.3 million people by the year 2000. Idaho's new businesses and beautiful land and waters keep drawing them in.

Idaho celebrated its 100th birthday in 1990.

Overleaf: A girl tending lambs near Twin Falls

25

Idahoans and Their Work

IDAHOANS AND THEIR WORK

*I*n 1990, Idaho had just over 1 million people. It is a fast-growing state. Yet, only eight states have fewer people. About 95 of every 100 Idahoans are white. Long ago, most of their families came from England, Germany, and Ireland. The state's 55,000 Hispanics are its largest minority. Most of these Idahoans have Mexican backgrounds. Idaho has about 14,000 American Indians. Many of them live on Idaho's four federal reservations. Others live in other parts of the state. The Nez Percé, Shoshone, and Bannock are major tribes today. The Gem State is home to 10,000 Asian Americans. Many of them are Japanese Americans. Only 3,500 black Americans live in Idaho.

About 55,000 Hispanics live in Idaho, and about 10,000 Asian Americans.

IDAHOANS AT WORK

About 450,000 Idahoans have jobs. Selling goods is their leading type of work. More than 100,000 Idahoans sell goods. These goods range from hamburgers to snowmobiles. Albertson's is a large grocery chain. It is based in Boise. There are about 700 Albertson's stores in nineteen states.

White Cloud Mountain Coffee is roasted at this Boise company.

This farmer in northeast Idaho is testing barley.

Idaho has about 100,000 service workers. Many are health-care workers. Others work in motels and at other jobs that serve tourists. In 1993, tourists spent $1.7 billion in Idaho. Another 85,000 Idahoans are government workers. They include workers in Idaho's fifteen national forests and twenty-two state parks.

About 63,000 Idahoans make or package goods. Foods are their top product. Many fresh and frozen potatoes are packaged in Idaho. Sugar and meats are other Idaho foods. Wooden goods are made with Idaho lumber. Computers and chemicals are also made in the Gem State.

Farming employs more than 35,000 Idahoans. The state's top crop is potatoes. Idaho leads all the states at growing potatoes. Idaho ranks second at growing sugar beets and lentils. It is third at growing barley. Wheat, hay, apples, plums, peas, and snap beans are other Idaho crops. Beef cattle are the state's top livestock product. Idaho's dairy cows give much milk. Much wool comes from its sheep. The state ranks first at raising pond-farmed trout.

More than 3,000 Idahoans work in mining. About 600,000 pounds of silver a year comes from Idaho mines. Only Nevada mines more. Silver is used in jewelry, photography, tooth fillings, and silver-

ware. Idaho is the top state for mining vanadium and antimony. They are metals. Vanadium is used to strengthen steel. Antimony is used in printing. Phosphate is another major Idaho mining product. It is used to make fertilizer. Lead is Idaho's major metal product. Gold and copper are also mined in the state. So is zinc, which goes into pennies. More than eighty kinds of gemstones are found in the Gem State. They include garnets and opals.

A cattle roundup near Mackay

Overleaf: A view of the Sawtooth Mountains from Little Redfish Lake

29

A Gem State Tour

A Gem State Tour

*I*dahoans and visitors enjoy the Gem State's mountains, rivers, and lakes. They ski, snowmobile, and go white-water rafting. Some people learn about Idaho's early history in its small towns. Larger towns add to the Gem State's sparkle.

Idaho has over 3,000 miles of white-water rivers. That's more than any other state.

Boise, Capital and Largest City

French fur trappers reached a southwest Idaho river in the early 1800s. They called it *la rivière boissie.* Those are French words meaning "wooded river." A town was founded on its banks in 1863. The town was named Boise for the river. Boise's nickname is "City of Trees." Today, Boise is Idaho's largest city.

Boise has been Idaho's capital since 1864. Idaho lawmakers meet in the State Capitol. It was finished in 1920. This domed building looks like the United States Capitol in Washington, D.C. Boise schoolchildren placed the Pioneer Monument on the capitol grounds. It honors the pioneers who used the Oregon Trail.

Boise is home to the Idaho Historical Museum. Visitors can see what pioneer homes and an old

Boise

The Idaho capitol

saloon looked like. The Basque Museum tells about Boise's Basque people. In the 1800s, thousands of Basques came to Idaho. They were from the Pyrenees Mountains between Spain and France. Many Idaho Basques became sheepherders. Each December, Boise hosts the Sheepherder's Ball. Basques wear colorful costumes and play their folk music at the ball. Visitors to the Old Idaho Penitentiary learn about Idaho's lawmen and outlaws. This building housed prisoners for 103 years. In 1973 it closed. Several museums are on the prison grounds. The Transportation Museum is one of them. It shows how people have traveled in

Basque dancers

Idaho over the years. Zoo Boise is another highlight of the city. At its petting zoo, children and animals can become friends.

OTHER SOUTHWEST IDAHO HIGHLIGHTS

Birds of prey eat other animals.

Rodeo riders at the Snake River Stampede

The Snake River Birds of Prey Natural Area is south of Boise. It has the largest nesting place on earth of eagles and hawks. Prairie falcons and owls also fly about.

Nampa is west of Boise. With more than 28,000 people, it is Idaho's fourth-biggest city. The Amalgamated Sugar Company is there. It is the largest sugar refinery in the United States. Each day, the company processes 24 million pounds of sugar beets. They become 3.2 million pounds of packaged sugar. Each July, Nampa hosts the Snake River Stampede. It is one of the most popular rodeos in Idaho.

Silver City is a ghost town south of Nampa. It was founded in 1863. Silver City was once a center for extremely rich gold and silver mines. By 1912, the town was pretty much closed down. Today, Silver City's shops, old hotel, and schoolhouse still stand. But the town is home to only four people each winter.

Twin Falls lies to the southeast. It is a city of about 28,000 people. It was once in the middle of a desert. Now, Twin Falls is known for farming. The Twin Falls Historical Museum tells how irrigation made the land bloom. Just north of town is the Perrine Bridge. It stands nearly 500 feet above the Snake River. Balanced Rock is west of Twin Falls. This is a 40-foot-high rock. Its tiny base hardly seems strong enough to hold it up. Shoshone Falls is to the north. It drops 212 feet over a rim on the Snake River.

In 1974, Evel Knievel attempted to jump a jet-powered motorcycle across the Snake River not far from the Perrine Bridge. He failed but lived to tell the tale.

Left: Silver City
Right: Balanced Rock

SOUTHEAST IDAHO

Minnetonka Cave is near the state's southeast corner. Its rooms look like palace halls. Dripping water made the cave's strange shapes. Thousands of bats hang from the cave's ceilings.

Lava Hot Springs is north of Minnetonka Cave. The springs are 50 million years old. Hot mineral waters bubble from them at 110 degrees Fahrenheit. Idaho's early Indians set the springs

Lava Hot Springs, downtown

aside for all Indians to share. Today, Lava Hot Springs is a resort. People come from all over to bathe and swim in the spring waters.

Pocatello is a short drive north from Lava Hot Springs. Begun in 1882, the town today has about 46,000 people. It is Idaho's second-biggest city. Old Fort Hall was rebuilt in Pocatello. Visitors can get an idea about life at an 1830s trading post. Pocatello is also home to Idaho State University (ISU). The Idaho Museum of Natural History is at ISU. Fossils of animals that once lived in Idaho can be seen there. The museum also has Indian spear points and arrowheads. Some date back 10,000 years.

To the north lies the Fort Hall Indian Reservation. Each summer, the Shoshone-Bannock Indian Festival takes place there. Visitors can enjoy Indian foods and dances.

Idaho Falls is Idaho's third-biggest city. It is north of the Indian reservation. About 44,000 people live there. Idaho Falls has forty parks. That's quite a few for a city its size. Tautphaus Park is home to the Idaho Falls Zoo. People go there to see monkeys, zebras, and big cats. The Idaho Vietnam Memorial is in Freeman Park. More than 200 Idahoans died in the Vietnam War.

A dancer at the Shoshone-Bannock Indian Festival

The Idaho Vietnam Memorial in Idaho Falls

This 700-foot-high cone can be seen at Craters of the Moon National Monument.

CENTRAL IDAHO

Craters of the Moon National Monument is west of Idaho Falls. Lava started flowing out of the ground there 15,000 years ago. The lava hardened into odd shapes. Today, visitors explore craters, caves, and cones there.

To the northwest is Sun Valley. In 1936, Averell Harriman began a ski resort there. Harriman was an owner of the Union Pacific Railroad. Today, Sun Valley's ski runs draw people from around the world.

Sawtooth National Recreation Area is north of Sun Valley. It covers 1,200 square miles. The state of Rhode Island could fit inside it. The Sawtooth Mountains are west of the Rockies. They rise over the recreation area. More than 300 lakes nestle in the mountains. Black bears, elk, mountain goats, and mountain lions roam about. A few wolves do, too. Visitors there enjoy outdoor fun year-round. Hiking, rafting, and cross-country skiing are a few activities.

Challis is north of the Sawtooth National Recreation Area. Each spring, Challis hosts the

Riders on the trail at Sawtooth National Recreation Area

Rafters on the Salmon River

Lewiston is the farthest inland seaport in the West. It's part of the Columbia-Snake River Inland Waterway.

Little Britches Rodeo. Young people ages eight to eighteen can enter. Challis began as a supply center for gold and silver miners. The ghost towns of Bonanza and Custer are nearby. The Custer Museum is in an old one-room school. It displays gold ore and miners' tools.

Salmon lies where the Salmon and Lemhi rivers join. Sacagawea, Lewis and Clark's Shoshone interpreter, was born near Salmon. The Lemhi County Historical Museum is in Salmon. Displays on Indian life and gold mining can be seen there.

Hells Canyon is across the state from Salmon. It helps form the Idaho-Oregon border. Hells Canyon is the deepest canyon in North America. The Snake River carved it to a depth of 1.5 miles. Visitors can reach the canyon's bottom by car, but they have to continue downstream on foot or horseback. Others reach Hells Canyon by boat on the Snake River.

NORTHERN IDAHO

Lewiston is in northwest Idaho. It is on the Idaho-Washington border. Lewiston was laid out in 1861. It was named for Meriwether Lewis. Idaho's lowest point is at Lewiston. The Snake River there lies just 710 feet above sea level. From 1863 to 1864,

Lewiston was the Idaho Territory's first capital. Today, it is northern Idaho's largest city. More than 28,000 people live there. Each spring, Lewiston hosts the Dogwood Festival. A children's Bike, Trike, and Hike Parade is part of the fun.

To the east is Orofino. Each fall, Orofino holds Lumberjack Days. It honors Idaho's old-time lumberjacks. Events include log-chopping contests.

Moscow is north of Lewiston. The University of Idaho is there. It was founded in 1889. The Appaloosa Horse Museum is also at Moscow. There, visitors can learn how the Nez Percé bred this horse.

The University of Idaho administration building

A view of Lewiston

An inside view of Cataldo Mission

The Nez Perce Reservation is between Lewiston, Orofino, and Kooskia. The Heart of the Monster is on the reservation. This is a rock formation. The Indians say it was once a monster's heart. Blood from the heart became the Nez Percé people. The town of Spalding is on the reservation. A Nez Percé museum is there. Visitors can see Nez Percé clothing, tools, and toys.

Northernmost Idaho is called the Panhandle. Its shape is like a pan's handle. Lake Coeur d'Alene is in the Panhandle. It is one of the world's loveliest lakes. People sail and fish on Lake Coeur d'Alene. It is home to the largest number of ospreys in the western United States. These birds make high dives into the water to catch fish. Coeur d'Alene is a city on the lake. The Museum of North Idaho is there. It is a good place to learn about the Panhandle's logging industry.

Cataldo Mission is east of Coeur d'Alene. Father Anthony Ravalli and Coeur d'Alene Indians built it in the 1850s. Cataldo Mission is Idaho's oldest building. It is also one of its handsomest.

Farther east is Kellogg. In 1885, Noah Kellogg found a rich silver and lead vein there. It became the Bunker Hill and Sullivan Mine. Its total production makes it the country's largest lead and silver

mine. Nearby is the mining town of Wallace. Visitors can tour the Sierra Silver Mine. It is an old, abandoned mine.

Lake Pend Oreille is in the middle of the Panhandle. Mountains circle the lake, adding to its beauty. Many kinds of fish swim in the lake. The largest bull trout anywhere was fished from its waters in 1949. The giant fish weighed thirty-two pounds.

Moyie Falls is a good place to end an Idaho tour. This waterfall is near the Canadian border. The Moyie River tumbles through a canyon to form Moyie Falls. It splashes over the falls. Sometimes the water looks like millions of pieces of colored glass.

Left: A yacht harbor at Coeur d'Alene
Right: Cataldo Mission

Overleaf: Senator William E. Borah

43

A Gallery
of Famous
Idahoans

A Gallery of Famous Idahoans

Many Idahoans have won fame. They include lawmakers, athletes, and authors.

William E. Borah (1865-1940) was born in Illinois. He moved to Boise in 1890. He became a great Boise lawyer. In 1907, Borah served Idaho as a U.S. senator (1907-1940). Senator Borah was a major supporter of the Kellogg-Briand Pact (1928). It tried to end all wars. Idaho's tallest mountain, Borah Peak, was named for him.

Gutzon Borglum (1867-1941) was born near Bear Lake. He became a great sculptor. His best-known work is the giant Mount Rushmore Memorial. It is in South Dakota's Black Hills. Borglum carved the heads of four presidents on the mountainside. They are Presidents Washington, Jefferson, Lincoln, and Theodore Roosevelt.

Ezra Taft Benson (1899-1994) was born on his family's farm at Whitney. Reportedly, he drove a team of horses by the age of five. Benson became an Idaho farm economist and Boise church leader. He belonged to many farming groups throughout the state and country. Later, he served as U.S. secretary

Statues of William Borah and George Shoup (Idaho's first state governor) stand in the Capitol in Washington, D.C.

Ezra Taft Benson

of agriculture (1953-1961). In 1985, Benson became president of the Mormon Church. He held that post until his death.

Gracie Bowers Pfost (1906-1965) was born in Arkansas. Her family moved to a farm near Boise a few years later. In 1950, Pfost ran for the U.S. House of Representatives. She lost. But she tried again in 1952 and won. Pfost served as Idaho's first woman in the U.S. House of Representatives (1953-1963). She played a key role in making Alaska the forty-ninth state in 1959.

Philo T. Farnsworth (1906-1971) was born in Utah. He moved to Rigby as a young boy. As a six-teen-year-old high-school student, Farnsworth developed the image dissector. It was an invention that led to the creation of television.

Joe Albertson (1906-1993) was born in Okla-homa. His family moved to Caldwell when he was about three. He worked as a janitor while at the College of Idaho in Caldwell. But Albertson had to leave college. He didn't have enough money. He went to work as a grocery-store clerk. In 1939, Albertson opened his own grocery store in Boise. Albertson's featured "Big Joe" ice-cream cones. Joe built Albertson's into a giant chain. He also gave much time and money to the College of Idaho. In

1991, it was named Albertson College of Idaho in his honor.

Jack Simplot was born in Iowa in 1909. His family moved to a farm near Declo when he was two. As a young man, Simplot rented land near Declo. On it, he grew potatoes. Simplot became the country's largest shipper of fresh potatoes. In the 1950s, Simplot pioneered the frozen french fry. Today, the J. R. Simplot Company is based in Boise. It is one of the world's largest frozen potato makers. Jack Simplot is a billionaire. He's called "Mr. Spud" around Boise.

Joseph Garry (1910-1976) was born on Idaho's Coeur d'Alene Reservation. He taught sev-

Left: Gracie Bowers Pfost
Right: Joseph Garry

The J. R. Simplot Company provides two-thirds of the frozen french fries used by McDonald's in the United States.

enth grade there. Garry also became a famous leader. For about twenty years, he was the Coeur d'Alene tribal chairman. He also served as president of the National Congress of American Indians. This is the country's largest American Indian group. In 1956, Garry was elected a state representative. He became the first American Indian in Idaho's legislature. Joseph Garry worked in many ways to improve American Indians' lives. Twice he was named Outstanding Indian of North America.

Julia (Lana) Turner was born in Wallace in 1920. When she was fifteen, Turner signed a movie

Left: Lana Turner
Right: Ezra Pound

contract. But she was told to pick a new first name. Julia chose the name Lana. Lana Turner became one of the world's most glamorous stars. Her movies include *Ziegfeld Girl* and *Johnny Eager.*

Several great writers were Idahoans. **Ezra Pound** (1885-1972) was born in Hailey. But he spent most of his life in Europe. Pound took fifty years writing *The Cantos.* Their 800 pages talk of history, government, and correct behavior. Pound has been called modern poetry's most important writer.

Ernest Hemingway

Carol Ryrie Brink (1895-1981) was born in Moscow, Idaho. Her parents died when she was a child. Brink's grandmother, Caddie Woodhouse, raised her. "How I loved the stories of her pioneer childhood!" Brink later recalled. Brink became a children's author. Her best-known book is *Caddie Woodlawn.* It tells of her grandmother's life. This novel won the 1936 Newbery Medal.

Vardis Fisher (1895-1968) was born in Annis. He wrote the *Idaho Guide.* It is one of the best books about the Gem State's people and places. Fisher also wrote novels. *The Children of God* is one about the Mormons. **Ernest Hemingway** (1899-1961) was born in Illinois. This great writer often visited Sun Valley. Hemingway worked on *For*

Frank Church

Cecil Andrus

Whom the Bell Tolls in Idaho. In 1954, he won the Nobel Prize for literature. Hemingway spent his last years in Ketchum.

Frank Church (1924-1984) was born in Boise. Church won a national speaking contest as a teenager. Later, he served as a U.S. senator from Idaho (1957-1981). Senator Church was a leading opponent of the Vietnam War. He worked on behalf of U.S. schools and the elderly. Church also worked to protect Idaho's land and waters. The Frank Church River of No Return Wilderness Area is named for him.

Cecil Andrus was born in Oregon. Later, he moved to Idaho. Andrus served as Idaho's governor (1971-1977 and 1987-1994). Between his terms as governor, Andrus was U.S. secretary of the interior (1977-1981). As secretary and governor, he worked to protect Idaho's land and waters. Governor Andrus worked to improve the lives of young Idahoans. He declared the 1990s the "Decade of the Child."

Larry EchoHawk was born in Wyoming in 1948. He is a Pawnee Indian. In 1978, he moved to Idaho. There, he served as lawyer for the Shoshone and Bannock Indians. EchoHawk soon entered government. In 1991, he became Idaho's attorney general. EchoHawk was the first American Indian attorney general of any state.

Two baseball greats were Idaho natives. **Vernon Law** was born in 1930 in Meridian. He played sixteen years with the Pittsburgh Pirates. Law won 162 games. In 1960, he won the Cy Young Award as baseball's best pitcher. **Harmon Killebrew** was born in Payette in 1936. He had an after-school job painting houses. It helped build up his arms and wrists. Later, Killebrew became a great hitter. He led the Minnesota Twins to three championships. He won six home-run crowns. He is fifth on the all-

As a Mormon elder, Vern Law would preach at a local Mormon church wherever his team was playing on a Sunday.

Harmon Killebrew

time list with 573 homers. Killebrew is also in the Baseball Hall of Fame. Both Law and Killebrew are Mormons.

Two Idahoans became football stars. **Jerry Kramer** was born in Montana in 1936. Later, he moved to Idaho. Kramer went to high school in Sandpoint. He attended the University of Idaho. Kramer became an offensive lineman and kicker for the Green Bay Packers. He helped the Pack win five championships. **Larry Wilson** was born in 1938 in Rigby. He is known as the "Toughest Man in Pro Football." He had fifty-two career interceptions. Wilson was elected to the Pro Football Hall of Fame in 1978.

Liz Paul was born in California in 1957. She taught skiing near Ketchum. Paul learned that the test station near Arco was polluting Idaho waters. She then began fighting nuclear pollution. Paul worked with a group called the Snake River Alliance. In 1986, the group helped stop the production of atomic weapons in Idaho. Today, the Snake River Alliance fights shipping of nuclear wastes into Idaho.

Barbara Morgan was born in California in 1951. For many years she has taught third grade in McCall, Idaho. In 1985, Morgan was chosen for the

Teacher in Space Program. One day she may fly aboard a U.S. space shuttle. She could become the first teacher in space.

Barbara Morgan

The birthplace of Carol Ryrie Brink, Joseph Garry, Frank Church, and Lana Turner . . .

Home, too, to Gracie Bowers Pfost, Cecil Andrus, Larry EchoHawk, and Barbara Morgan . . .

The site of Craters of the Moon National Monument, Shoshone Falls, and Hells Canyon . . .

Number one in growing potatoes, and a top producer of sugar beets, lumber, and silver . . .

This is Idaho—the Gem State!

Did You Know?

Nampa was named for the Paiute chief Nampuh. Pocatello was named for a Shoshone chief.

Shoshone Ice Caves and Crystal Ice Cave are in southern Idaho. They were formed in lava beds.

Edgar Rice Burroughs reportedly wrote the first drafts of *Tarzan of the Apes* while running a store in Pocatello.

Idaho has places named Chilly, Bone, Deary, Squirrel, and Sunbeam.

In 1986, fifteen-year-old Tonya Mistal set a record for Hula-Hoop twirling at Ted's Burgers in Moscow, Idaho. She kept the hoop twirling around her waist for eighty-eight hours.

Elephant-like mammoths and mastodons roamed Idaho during the Ice Age. Long ago, Idaho was also home to saber-toothed tigers. These 400-pound wild cats had teeth like swords.

The Silent City of Rocks is near Almo in far southern Idaho. The area is made up of huge granite columns shaped by wind and water. It looks somewhat like an ancient city's skyline. Reportedly, a fortune in gold from an 1878 stagecoach robbery is buried there.

The world's biggest women's bicycle race takes place in Idaho. The Powerbar International Women's Challenge covers several hundred miles. Women from around the world enter the race, which offers about $60,000 in prizes.

Idaho lies exactly halfway between the North Pole and the equator.

Three women achieved recent "firsts" on Idaho courts. In 1990, Cathy Silak was named the first woman judge on Idaho's Court of Appeals. In 1992, Linda Copple Trout was appointed as the first woman judge on the Idaho Supreme Court. That year, Ida Leggett became Idaho's first black judge.

Mullan Pass holds Idaho's record for snow depth. In February 1954, the snow lay 15 feet deep at this northern Idaho mountain pass.

If all the potatoes that Idaho grows in a year were placed end to end, they would stretch nearly 2 million miles. That's about eight times the distance between the earth and the moon.

IDAHO INFORMATION

State flag

Mountain bluebird

Area: 83,574 square miles (the thirteenth-biggest state)

Greatest Distance North to South: 483 miles

Greatest Distance East to West: 316 miles

Borders: The country of Canada to the north; Montana and Wyoming to the east; Utah and Nevada to the south; Oregon and Washington to the west

Highest Point: Borah Peak, 12,662 feet above sea level

Lowest Point: The Snake River at Lewiston, 710 feet above sea level

Hottest Recorded Temperature: 118° F. (at Orofino, on July 28, 1934)

Coldest Recorded Temperature: -60° F. (at Island Park Dam, on January 18, 1943)

Statehood: The forty-third state, on July 3, 1890

Origin of Name: *Idaho* was coined by George Willing, who originally intended the name for the region that became known as Colorado

Capital: Boise

United States Representatives: 2

State Senators: 35

State Representatives: 70

State Song: "Here We Have Idaho," by Sallie Hume-Douglas (music) and McKinley Helm and Albert Tompkins (words)

State Motto: *Esto Perpetua* (Latin, meaning "Be Perpetual" or "It Must Last Forever")

Nicknames: "Gem State," "Gem of the Mountains," "Spud State"

State Seal: Adopted in 1891   **State Flag:** Adopted in 1907

State Flower: Syringa   **State Bird:** Mountain bluebird

State Tree: Western white pine   **State Horse:** Appaloosa

State Insect: Monarch butterfly   **State Fish:** Cutthroat trout

State Gemstone: Star garnet   **State Folk Dance:** Square dance

State Fossil: Hagerman horse fossil

Main Mountain System: Rocky Mountains

Some Mountains: Bitterroot, Salmon River, Sawtooth, Clearwater, Centennial, Coeur d'Alene

Some Rivers: Snake, Salmon, Kootenai, Pend Oreille, Clearwater, Payette, Bear, Big Lost, Boise

Some Lakes: Pend Oreille, Coeur d'Alene, Priest, Hayden, Payette, Bear, American Falls, Lucky Peak, Cascade

Wildlife: Black bears, grizzly bears, moose, caribou, white-tailed deer, elk, mountain goats, mountain lions, bobcats, bighorn sheep, coyotes, raccoons, beavers, foxes, wolves, badgers, porcupines, otters, pronghorn antelopes, prairie dogs, mountain bluebirds, hummingbirds, swans, bald eagles, golden eagles, ducks, geese, great blue herons, ospreys, many other kinds of birds, trout, salmon, whitefish, perch, bass, sturgeon

Farm Products: Potatoes, sugar beets, lentils, barley, wheat, hay, plums, apples, peas, snap beans, mint, beef cattle, milk, sheep, pond-farmed trout

Manufactured Products: Packaged potatoes, sugar, meat, other foods, fertilizers, other chemicals, lumber, wood products, computers, computer parts, farm machinery

Mining Products: Lead, silver, phosphate, gold, clays, molybdenum, vanadium, antimony, zinc, copper, garnet, opal, many other kinds of gemstones

Population: 1,006,749, forty-second among the states (1990 U.S. Census Bureau figures)

Major Cities (1990 Census):

Boise	125,738	Twin Falls	27,591
Pocatello	46,080	Coeur d'Alene	24,563
Idaho Falls	43,929	Moscow	18,519
Nampa	28,365	Caldwell	18,400
Lewiston	28,082	Rexburg	14,302

White pine tree

Monarch butterfly

Square dancers

IDAHO HISTORY

About 13,000 B.C.—The first people reach Idaho

1776—The United States of America is founded

1805—The Lewis and Clark Expedition explores Idaho for the United States

1807—John Colter, a mountain man, discovers what is now Yellowstone National Park

1809—David Thompson of the English North West Company builds Kullyspell House, Idaho's first non-Indian structure

1834—Fort Hall and Fort Boise, two trading posts, are built

1836—Missionaries Henry and Eliza Spalding, Idaho's first permanent non-Indian settlers, open a mission at Lapwai

1855—Mormons build Lemhi, a mission settlement

1860—Mormons begin Franklin, which is now Idaho's oldest town; Elias Pierce finds gold in northern Idaho

1861—Lewiston is laid out

1862—The *Golden Age,* Idaho's first newspaper, is published in Lewiston; Idaho City is founded

1863—U.S. soldiers kill nearly 400 Shoshones in the Bear River Massacre; Boise is founded; the Idaho Territory is established with Lewiston as its capital

1864—Boise becomes the Idaho Territory's capital

1874—The first railroad into Idaho arrives

1877—Under Chief Joseph, the Nez Percé battle bravely but are defeated by U.S. soldiers in the Nez Percé War

1878—The Bannocks are defeated in the Bannock War

1889—Idaho adopts the state constitution that is in use to the present day; the University of Idaho is founded

1890—On July 3, Idaho becomes the forty-third state

1892—Fighting occurs between union miners and mine owners in the Coeur d'Alene region

A horse-drawn wagon at Ketchum's annual Ore Wagon Days Parade

1899—Governor Frank Steunenberg calls in U.S. soldiers to end a miners' strike

1901—Idaho State University is founded

1905—Former governor Frank Steunenberg is murdered in revenge for earlier labor troubles

1910—A huge forest fire strikes northern Idaho, killing about eighty-five people

1914—Moses Alexander becomes the first Jewish person elected as a full-term state governor

1917-18—Idaho's 22,000 troops help win World War I

1922—Philo Farnsworth invents television while a high-school student in Rigby

1929-39—The Great Depression hits the nation; Idaho's farmers, miners, and loggers are especially hard hit

1932—Boise State University begins as a junior college

1936—Sun Valley is created as a major ski resort

1941-45—Idaho sends 65,000 men and women, plus food and metals, to help win World War II

1949—The United States sets up the National Reactor Testing Station near Arco

1959—Palisades Dam, one of many Idaho irrigation projects, is completed on the Snake River

1972—A fire in the Sunshine Silver Mine kills ninety-one people

1976—The collapse of Teton Dam kills eleven and causes $500 million in damages

1977—Idaho's Cecil Andrus becomes secretary of the interior

1983—A huge earthquake shakes the Borah Peak area

1987-88—A severe drought strikes Idaho

1990—On July 3, the Gem State is 100 years old

1994—Idahoans battle raging forest fires; the state produces a record potato crop

Frank Steunenberg

MAP KEY

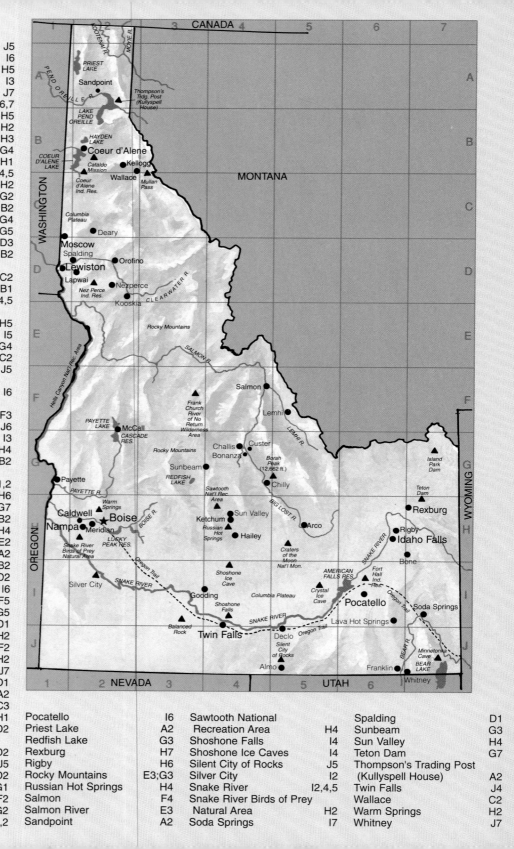

GLOSSARY

Appaloosa: The spotted horse bred by the Nez Percé

billion: A thousand million (1,000,000,000)

canyon: A deep, steep-sided valley

capital: The city that is the seat of government

capitol: The building in which the government meets

climate: An area's typical weather

decade: A ten-year period

depression: A period of very hard times with widespread joblessness

desert: A very dry region

drought: A period when rainfall is well below normal

endangered species: An animal or a plant threatened with being wiped out

explorer: A person who visits and studies unknown lands

fossil: The remains of animals or plants that lived long ago

glacier: A big, slowly moving sheet of ice

irrigation: The watering of land through canals and other artificial methods

million: A thousand thousand (1,000,000)

missionary: A person who leaves home to spread his or her religion in other lands

nuclear reactor: A machine that splits parts of atoms to produce electricity

pollute: To make dirty

population: The number of people in a place

reservoir: An artificially made lake where water is stored

sculptor: A person who makes statues and other three-dimensional artworks

territory: The name for a part of the United States before it became a state

tourism: The business of providing services such as food and lodging for visitors

volcano: A crack through which lava and other materials erupt; the mountain built by volcanic eruptions

Skiing in Sun Valley

PICTURE ACKNOWLEDGMENTS

Front cover, ©Brett Baunton/**Tony Stone Images, Inc.**; 1, ©Ric Ergenbright/**Tony Stone Images, Inc.**; 2, **Tom Dunnington**; 3, **©Steve Bly**; 5, **Tom Dunnington**; 6, ©Ric Ergenbright/**Tony Stone Images, Inc.**; 4 (left), **Courtesy of Hammond Incorporated, Maplewood, New Jersey**; 4 (right), ©David Muench/**Tony Stone Images, Inc.**; 8 (left), **©Steve Bly**; 8 (right), ©James Blank/**H. Armstrong Roberts**; 9, **©Steve Bly**; 10 (top), ©Steve Bly/**F-Stock, Inc.**; 10 (bottom), ©Joey Terra/**F-Stock, Inc.**; 11, ©D. Muench/**H. Armstrong Roberts**; 12-13, **Idaho State Historical Society #77-144-28**; 14, **©Steve Bly**; 15, **Idaho State Historical Society #63-221-125b**; 16, **Courtesy of the Montana Historical Society**; 17, **Stock Montage, Inc.**; 19, **Idaho State Historical Society #2247**; 21, **Idaho State Historical Society #61-43**; 22, **The Bettmann Archive**; 23, **UPI/Bettmann**; 24, **©Steve Bly**; 25, **©Steve Bly**; 26, ©Marc Auth/**N E Stock Photo**; 27 (top), ©Marc A. Auth/**N E Stock Photo**; 27 (bottom), ©Caroline Wood/**F-Stock, Inc.**; 28 (both pictures), **©Steve Bly**; 29, ©Gary Brettnacher/**SuperStock**; 30-31, ©Kirk Anderson/**F-Stock, Inc.**; 32, ©Steve Bly/**F-Stock, Inc.**; 33 (top), ©David Schultz/**Tony Stone Images, Inc.**; 33 (bottom), **©Steve Bly**; 34, ©John Blackmer/**Steve Bly**; 35 (left), ©Peter Pearson/**Tony Stone Images, Inc.**; 35 (right), **©Gene Ahrens**; 36, **©Steve Bly**; 37 (top), ©Mark W. Lisk/**F-Stock, Inc.**; 37 (bottom), **©Steve Bly**; 38, ©Peter Pearson/**Tony Stone Images, Inc.**; 39, **©Steve Bly**; 40, ©Steve Bly/**F-Stock, Inc.**; 41 (top), **©Steve Bly**; 41 (bottom), ©Steve Bly/**F-Stock, Inc.**; 42, ©Mark E. Gibson/**mga/Photri**; 43 (left), **©Bob & Suzanne Clemenz**; 43 (right), ©Terry Donnelly/**Tom Stack and Associates**; 44, **Historical Photograph Collection, University of Idaho Library, Moscow, Idaho**, slide #7-1-1; 45, **UPI/Bettmann**; 47 (both pictures), **AP/Wide World Photos**; 48 (left), **UPI/Bettmann**; 48 (right), **The Bettmann Archive**; 49, **UPI/Bettmann**; 50 (top), **UPI/Bettmann Newsphotos**; 50 (bottom), **AP/Wide World Photos**; 51, **UPI/Bettmann**; 53, **AP/Wide World Photos**; 54 (top), **The Bettmann Archive**; 54 (bottom), ©T. Maben/**Steve Bly**; 55 (background), Karen Kohn; 55 (bottom), ©Stuart Wong/**Steve Bly**; 56 (top), **Courtesy Flag Research Center, Winchester, Massachusetts 01890**; 56 (bottom), ©Esther Schmidt/**FOTOPIC/mga/Photri**; 57 (top), **©Jerry Hennen**; 57 (middle), ©Glenn Jahnke/**Root Resources**; 57 (bottom), ©Marc A. Auth/**N E Stock Photo**; 58, ©Marc A. Auth/**N E Stock Photo**; 59, **Idaho State Historical Society #13**; 60, **Tom Dunnington**; 62, ©David Stoecklein/**F-Stock, Inc.**; back cover, **©Steve Bly**

INDEX

Page numbers in boldface type indicate illustrations.

About the Author

Dennis Brindell Fradin is the author of 150 published children's books. His works for Childrens Press include the Young People's Stories of Our States series, the Disaster! series, and the Thirteen Colonies series. Dennis is married to Judith Bloom Fradin, who taught high-school and college English for many years. She is now Dennis's chief researcher. The Fradins are the parents of two sons, Anthony and Michael, and a daughter, Diana. Dennis graduated from Northwestern University in 1967 with a B.A. in creative writing, and has lived in Evanston, Illinois, since that year.